Scholastic Canada Biographies

CANADIAN HEROES

Maxine Trottier

illustrated by

Tony Meers

DISCARDED

Scholastic Canada Ltd.
Toronto New York London Auckland Sydney
Mexico City New Delhi Hong Kong Buenos Aires

For the Five Coves Volunteer Fire Department,
Newman's Cove, Newfoundland. Heroes all.
– M.T.

Photo Credits

Page 5: Fort Verchères, Library and Archives Canada C-084464
Page 9: (left) Courtesy of the City of Verchères; (right) War Poster Collection, Rare Books and Special Collections Division, McGill University Libraries, Montreal, Canada
Page 10: (centre) Edward Tucker, Library and Archives Canada PA-160721; (lower) Library and Archives Canada C-056826
Page 13: Library and Archives Canada PA-123220
Page 14: (left) Library and Archives Canada PA-160591; (right) Library and Archives Canada PA-160723
Page 15: (left) National Film Board of Canada/Library and Archives Canada PA-114782; (right) Geza Karpathi, Library and Archives Canada C-067451
Page 17: Library and Archives Canada PA-161840
Page 18: National Film Board, Library and Archives Canada PA-114795
Page 19: Courtesy of Roderick Stewart
Page 25: Christopher J. Woods, Canadian Department of National Defence, Library and Archives Canada PA-142288
Page 26: (left) Maj. G.A. Flint, Company Commander of the 2nd Battalion, Princess Patricia Canadian Light Infantry, points out the next objective and briefs his officers and non-commissioned officers on the plan of attack. 11 Mar. 1951/Korea. © Department of National Defence. Reproduced with the permission of the Minister of Public Works and Government Services Canada (2006). Source: Library and Archives Canada/Department of National Defence Collection/Credit: Bill Olson/PA-114890; (right) © The Manitoba Museum
Page 27: Courtesy of the Historic Resources Branch, Manitoba Culture, Heritage and Tourism
Page 30: Courtesy of Roberta Bondar
Page 31: National Aeronautics and Space Administration S91-49534
Page 32: National Aeronautics and Space Administration S042-201-009
Page 33: National Aeronautics and Space Administration S42-79-00R
Page 35: (upper) National Aeronautics and Space Administration S91-51633; (lower) National Aeronautics and Space Administration S42-S-002
Pages 36, 38, 41, 42, 43, 44: Copyright © The Terry Fox Foundation
Page 45: Jeff Bassett/Canadian Press
Page 46: Canadian Press

Every effort has been made to obtain permission for, and to credit appropriately, all photographs used in this book. Any further information will be appreciated and acknowledged in subsequent editions.

The author and editor wish to thank Parks Canada, Bill Shead, Christine Yankou, Roberta Bondar, Doug Alward, Rick Hansen and the Fox family for their thoughtful assistance.

Library and Archives Canada Cataloguing in Publication

Trottier, Maxine
Canadian heroes / Maxine Trottier ; Tony Meers, illustrator.

(Scholastic Canada biographies)
ISBN-13: 978-0-439-94898-2
ISBN-10: 0-439-94898-3

1. Heroes--Canada--Biography--Juvenile literature.
2. Canada--Biography--Juvenile literature. I. Meers, Tony
II. Title. III. Series.
FC25.T763 2007   j920.071   C2006-904657-3

6 5 4 3 2 1   Printed in Canada   07 08 09 10 11

Contents

Madeleine de Verchères

The Brave Defender

On March 3, 1678, a baby girl named Marie Madeleine was born in New France.

The early years of the colony had been difficult ones. The Iroquois resented the French who had settled, unasked, on their lands. They attacked, and in 1665 the Carignan-Salières Regiment was sent over from France to defend the colony. Once the Iroquois had been subdued, some of the soldiers decided to remain. One of them, 24-year-old François Jarret, married Marie Perrot, a girl of 12 and a half. The couple was granted a seigneury, a narrow strip of land that ran one *lieue* (3.3 kilometres) from the south shore of the St. Lawrence River.

It was here at Verchères, 40 kilometres from Montreal, that François and Marie began to raise a family and farm the land. Little did they know how brave and resourceful Marie Madeleine, their fourth child, would turn out to be.

By the time Madeleine was 14, the seigneury had doubled in size and included 11 *habitant* families, with 50 hectares under cultivation. Madeleine's father, the seigneur, had 8 hectares of farmland, with 13 head of cattle. A rectangular palisade over four metres high surrounded the manor house and other buildings. One building served as a guardhouse and a place to store weapons and ammunition. The single gate facing the river made the stockade a secure fort.

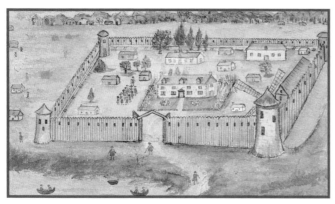

A depiction of
Fort Verchères

On October 2, 1692, Madeleine's parents were both away. Most of the soldiers who protected the settlement were off hunting. At eight o'clock in the morning, Madeleine was outside the palisade when she heard the firing of muskets. An Iroquois war party was attacking the *habitants* some distance away. Madeleine turned and sped toward the fort, with the warriors firing their muskets as she ran. Other *habitants* fled in the direction of Montreal. Nearing

the gates, Madeleine shouted, "To arms! To arms!" urging la Bonté and Galhet, the two soldiers who were inside, to come to the fort's defence.

She shooed in two women who were crying over their husbands and closed the gates. She knew she must act quickly to protect those inside: an old man of 80, the women and the children, including her younger brothers Pierre and Alexandre. Several of the palisade's posts had fallen down. She would later write, "I seized one end of the heavy stake and urged my companions to give a hand in raising it."

Madeleine then hurried to the guardhouse. One of the soldiers was huddled on the floor. The other held a burning fuse. He planned to set it to the gunpowder and blow up the fort. Furious, Madeleine scolded them. She took off her cap and put a soldier's *chapeau* on her head. Picking up a musket, she urged the soldiers and her brothers to fight. They took to their guns, and then she ordered the cannon to be fired to alarm the Iroquois and to alert the neighbouring forts.

To avoid giving the impression that they were helpless, Madeleine silenced the women who were wailing over those caught outside the walls. As she was doing so, she saw a canoe coming down the

river. In it were unsuspecting friends, Pierre Fontaine and his family. When the two soldiers refused to help, Madeleine, armed with her musket, marched down to the river to bring them to safety.

That night a cold northeast wind began to blow. Hail and snow fell from the sky. Fearing another attack, Madeleine told Fontaine and the soldiers to take the women and children to the guardhouse, since it was the safest place. Then she, her brothers and the old man took up positions on the bastions at the four corners of the stockade. Every few minutes they would call out into the darkness, "All's well!" – hoping to convince the Iroquois that the fort was filled with soldiers.

Did the siege last for eight days, as one of Madeleine de Verchères's written accounts states? What seems certain is that she led her companions as they defended the fort, and that she went long hours without food or sleep.

At last a party of 40 soldiers arrived from Montreal. The Iroquois, seeing then that there was no possibility of taking the fort, hastily departed with 20 prisoners who were later released.

When Madeleine de Verchères's father died in 1700, she was only 22. Because of her courageous leadership eight years before, his military pension was transferred to her. In 1706 she married and moved to Sainte-Anne-de-la-Pérade, on the north shore of the St. Lawrence. She died there at the age of 69, and was buried on August 8, 1747.

For 200 years after her death, her bravery seemed to go unrecognized. Then, in 1911, the Canadian sculptor Louis-Philippe Hébert was commissioned by the government to create a statue to honour her. On September 21, 1913, the larger-than-life figure of Madeleine was unveiled in a ceremony at Verchères, Quebec. It has been called "Canada's Statue of Liberty." In 1922 the first French-Canadian feature-length movie, *Madeleine de*

Verchères, was filmed, and later her image was used on a World War II Canadian recruitment poster. To this day Madeleine de Verchères remains a symbol of courage, especially the courage of the people of New France.

Madeleine Jarret keeps watch over the town of Verchères.

Madeleine stands guard on a WW II poster.

MADELEINE DE VERCHÈRES · 1678-1747

NÉE à Sorel, l'héroïne nationale du Canada français. Le 22 octobre 1692, à l'âge de 14 ans et demi, avec l'aide de ses deux frères âgés de 12 et de 10 ans respectivement, elle défendit avec succès le Fort de Verchères contre 45 Iroquois. Elle symbolise l'héroïsme féminin de la Nouvelle-France. Décédée à Sainte-Anne de la Pérade.

HIER

AUJOURD'HUI

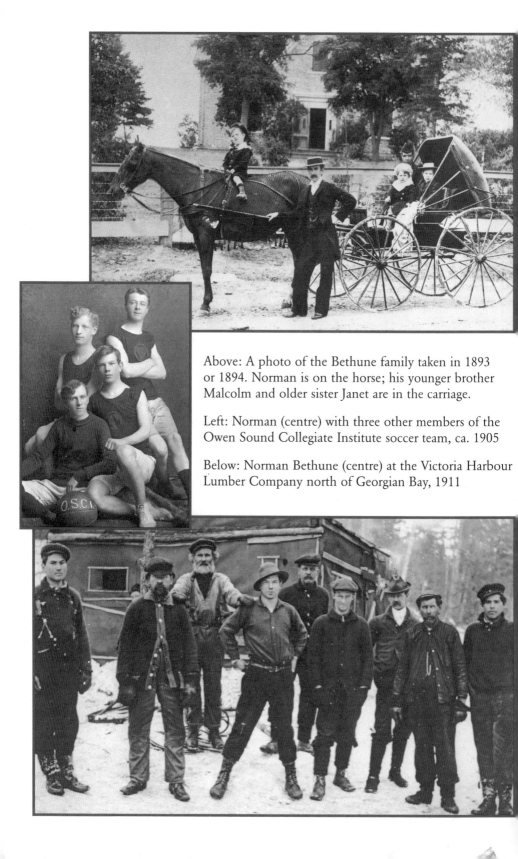

Above: A photo of the Bethune family taken in 1893 or 1894. Norman is on the horse; his younger brother Malcolm and older sister Janet are in the carriage.

Left: Norman (centre) with three other members of the Owen Sound Collegiate Institute soccer team, ca. 1905

Below: Norman Bethune (centre) at the Victoria Harbour Lumber Company north of Georgian Bay, 1911

Norman Bethune
The Selfless Healer

Henry Norman Bethune was born in Gravenhurst, Ontario, on March 3, 1890. His father, Malcolm, was a Presbyterian minister, and whenever he was assigned to a new church, the family moved with him.

When Norman was three, they settled in Toronto. He was a curious and independent child. Once, at the age of six, he set out to explore the city on his own. At the age of ten, he nearly drowned trying to swim across the harbour. Determined to succeed, he completed the crossing the next year. His father sometimes worried about the risks Norman took, but his mother, Elizabeth Ann, once said, "He must learn to take chances, so let him do what he wants and learn that way."

The Bethunes moved to Owen Sound, where Norman graduated from high school. In 1909 he enrolled at the University of Toronto. After two years he interrupted his science studies to work with men in an isolated lumber camp in northern Ontario – as a lumberjack and a teacher. He entered medical school at U of T in 1912, but when Canada entered the First World War in 1914, he immediately enlisted as a stretcher-bearer.

Badly wounded by shrapnel at the Second Battle of Ypres in Belgium, Norman spent six months in hospital before being sent home to Canada. Returning to medical school, he graduated in December 1916. Then he re-enlisted and served as a surgeon in the British navy and as a medical officer with Canadian airmen in France.

After the war Norman Bethune interned at the Fever Hospital and the Hospital for Children in London, England. He supported himself partly through buying and selling art. In 1923 he became

Bethune (back row, third from left) with other resident staff at the Great Ormond Street Hospital for Children in London, England, 1919

a Fellow of the Royal College of Surgeons in Edinburgh, Scotland, and married Frances Campbell Penney. They travelled through western Europe where he observed the work of surgeons.

In 1924 the Bethunes moved to Detroit, Michigan, in the United States, where Dr. Bethune opened a practice. Wealthy people began to come to him for treatment, often paying lavishly. Bethune, though, saw how poverty affected some of his patients, and worried about those who could not afford help. He believed in fairness for everyone. "Charity should be abolished and replaced by justice," he once said.

After only two years of practising medicine, Bethune was diagnosed with tuberculosis, an infectious disease, and confined to a sanatorium at Saranac Lake, New York. After nine depressing months, he insisted on a risky surgical procedure on his left lung. Two months later he was released, his health restored. As a result of this experience, Bethune began working at a tuberculosis hospital in Ray Brook, New York. By 1929 he was specializing in chest surgery at the Royal Victoria Hospital in Montreal, Quebec. He developed new surgical techniques and instruments, and wrote articles sharing his ideas.

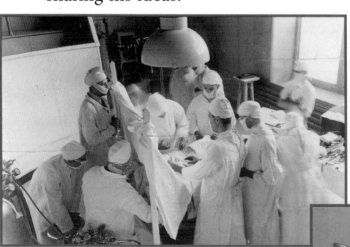

Left: Dr. Norman Bethune (facing camera) assists in an operation at the Royal Victoria Hospital in Montreal, 1933.

Below: Rib shears invented by Dr. Bethune, ca. 1930s

After visiting the Soviet Union in 1935, Bethune returned to Canada convinced that public health care was necessary. He joined the Communist Party of Canada and organized the Montreal Group for the Security of the People's Health, a group of doctors who believed in his ideas. "We take the medicine right down to the last individual," Dr. Bethune said.

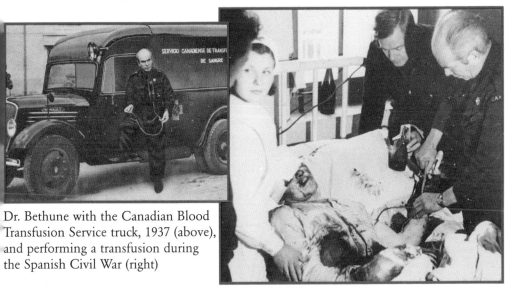

Dr. Bethune with the Canadian Blood Transfusion Service truck, 1937 (above), and performing a transfusion during the Spanish Civil War (right)

Then civil war broke out in Spain on July 17, 1936. Bethune, determined to help the Spanish people resist the military takeover, resigned from the hospital and sailed for Spain. Seeing dying soldiers filling the hospitals, he formed a plan. Buying a vehicle and stocking it with equipment, he created a mobile blood transfusion system that would bring blood to the wounded. Although he would later write, "Spain is a scar on my heart," he greatly reduced the number of deaths.

When he returned to Canada, he undertook a cross-country speaking tour to raise money for the Spanish cause. His tour was barely under way when Japan launched an attack on China. In a letter to Frances, Bethune said, "I am going to China because that is where I feel the need is greatest, that is where I can be most useful." Supported by donations, he left on January 2, 1938. After a difficult trip to reach the 8th Route Army and provide medical care, he found that there were no mobile medical services and began to organize them. The need he saw was terrible. The wounded and sick often had no beds or blankets, and barely any food. "Canada must help these people," he wrote home.

There were few doctors, so Bethune established more than 20 teaching and nursing hospitals to train staff. The mobile units followed the army, treating the wounded, and Bethune himself performed surgeries, once operating continuously for 69 hours on 115 people. He was sometimes ill, and loneliness plagued him, since there was only the translator to talk to. Bethune experienced great frustration. There

Students watch and learn as Dr. Bethune attends to wounded soldiers in China.

were never enough supplies and medicines, and it was often necessary for the doctors to donate their own blood for patients. Bethune typed letter after letter to friends in North America, often asking for assistance. Still, he knew he was doing his life's work. "I am tired," he wrote, "but enormously content."

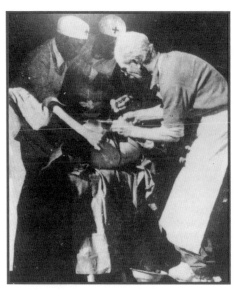

General Mao Zedong, a high-ranking Chinese officer, was greatly impressed by Bethune's selfless generosity. Bethune, whom the Chinese called *Bai Qiu-en*, had shared his food, clothing, and even his blood with both civilians and soldiers. In return he was offered the gratitude

Dr. Bethune performs surgery in an abandoned Buddhist temple, 1939.

and friendship of the Chinese people whom he was helping. On one occasion, after he had operated on a little boy and saved his life, the boy's father knelt on the ground to thank him.

Late in October 1939, Bethune cut his finger while operating bare-handed on a soldier's leg. A few days later, the cut became infected from another soldier's head wound. The poison spread through his exhausted body. There were no medicines that might have saved him, and he died of blood poisoning in a peasant's hut on November 12, 1939.

Mao Zedong, who later became chairman of the People's Republic of China, wrote an essay called, "In Memory of Norman Bethune." In it he said, "We must all learn the spirit of absolute selflessness from him." In the 1960s Mao's essay became required reading in China, Bethune's picture was used on posters and postage stamps, and statues of him were erected all over the country.

In time Canada honoured this dedicated man as well. Dr. Norman Bethune Collegiate Institute in Scarborough, Ontario, was named after him, as was Bethune College at York University in Toronto. His birthplace in Gravenhurst, now called Bethune Memorial House, is a national historic site. Two movies about his life have been filmed.

Dr. Norman Bethune was a tireless humanitarian who served people and helped where he was needed. He changed battlefield medicine forever, and is now recognized as one of Canada's selfless heroes.

One of the many statues erected in China to honour Dr. Norman Bethune

Tommy Prince

The Fearless Soldier

On October 15, 1915, an Ojibway baby was born in a canvas tent at Petersfield, Manitoba. He was a great-great-grandson of Peguis, the famous Saulteaux chief. His parents named him Thomas George Prince.

When Tommy was five years old, the growing family moved to Scanterbury on the Brokenhead Reserve north of Winnipeg. That year, Tommy went away to the Elkhorn Residential School, about 300 kilometres from the reserve.

Whenever he was home, he spent endless hours wandering the countryside. Taught by his father, he became a skilled tracker and marksman. He joined the army cadets. An expert shot, from a hundred metres away he could put five bullets through a target the size of a playing card. Tommy wanted to study law but the family had no money for that, so he went to work as a lumberjack when he was 16 years old. He hunted to feed the family, and sometimes worked as a farmhand.

Canada entered World War II in 1939. Tommy Prince enlisted the next year and joined the Royal Canadian Engineers. He later said, "As soon as I put on my uniform I felt a better man." After training, his unit sailed for England. Prince was promoted to lance corporal. He never let the men under him forget that he was a Native. When a letter arrived from his father, he would joke, "I've got a smoke signal from the chief."

In 1942 Prince volunteered to train as a paratrooper. He was promoted to sergeant, and before long, he was part of the 1st Special Service Force, a select Canadian/American unit composed of 1600 of the toughest men that could be found. This was the "Devil's Brigade," an elite group of soldiers who were trained to handle anything.

With them, Sergeant Prince had his courage tested during the Italian campaign. In February 1944 he volunteered for a dangerous mission. At night, acting alone, he ran a telephone wire one and a half kilometres into German territory to an abandoned farmhouse, where he could observe the enemy and

telephone back their exact locations. During the days of fighting that followed, however, the phone line was cut. Prince took off his uniform and put on some farmer's clothing that had been left in the house. Then he went out and weeded the field with a hoe until he found the break. Pretending to tie his shoelaces, he reconnected the wires. To avoid suspicion, he hoed more of the field before returning to the farmhouse to continue sending his reports.

That summer the Devil's Brigade entered France. In September Sergeant Prince scouted out German sites and hiked 70 kilometres through rugged mountains to report them. After this he was called to Buckingham Palace in London, England. There, King George VI pinned the Military Medal on his chest and, on behalf of President Roosevelt of the United States, awarded him the Silver Star.

When the war in Europe ended, Tommy Prince was sent back to Canada and was honourably discharged on June 15, 1945. He returned to the Brokenhead Reserve and worked as a lumberjack again. Dissatisfied with his life, he moved to Winnipeg, where he got work as a janitor. Using money supplied to war veterans by the Department of Veterans Affairs, he bought a panel truck and cleaning equipment. The next year, the Native people in Manitoba asked him to represent them before the government. They wanted changes to the Indian Act so that they would have better housing and schools. The work was frustrating, although Prince tried hard. When he returned to Winnipeg, he learned that a friend had smashed his truck and sold it. All his equipment had been sold, too. He returned to life as a lumberjack.

When North Korea invaded South Korea in 1950, Prince enlisted and joined the 2nd Battalion of the Princess Patricia's Canadian Light Infantry. He continued to perform many acts

Sgt. Tommy Prince shows his Military Medal to a fellow officer after the ceremony in London, England.

of bravery, though by this time he was suffering from painful arthritis in his knees. He returned to Canada to serve at Camp Borden, Ontario. When his legs improved, he volunteered for a second tour of duty in Korea, and was wounded in the right knee. After his return to Canada, he was honourably discharged a second time, on October 28, 1953. Praising his fellow soldiers he said, "They were a great bunch of guys. I'm here because they kept me safe and brought me home."

Above: Sgt. Tommy Prince's war medals

Left: Sgt. Prince (second from left) being briefed with other officers before setting out on patrols in Korea in 1951

Prince's personal life was often difficult. It was hard for a Native man, even one as decorated as he was, to get a good job. Yet in June of 1955, his heroism showed itself again when he rescued a drowning man from the Red River.

Tommy Prince spent his remaining years living quietly in Winnipeg. He died there at Deer Lodge Hospital on November 25, 1977. With his daughters Beryl and Beverly mourning him, he was buried at Brookside Cemetery with full military honours. More than 500 people — civilians and soldiers — were present, including Manitoba's Lieutenant Governor, The Honourable Francis Jobin, and diplomats from France, the United States and Italy. Six Princess Patricia's soldiers served as pallbearers. At the end of the service, five men from his home reserve chanted the song "Death of a Warrior."

Tommy Prince's bravery has been recognized in many ways. The Vancouver Island Military Museum at Nanaimo, B.C., has a special wall honouring him. There is a Sgt. Tommy Prince Street in Winnipeg, and a school has been named after him at the Brokenhead Reserve. The Government of Canada has established the "Sergeant Tommy Prince Army Training Initiative" for aboriginal recruiting, and the Tommy Prince Award is a scholarship created by the Assembly of First Nations.

For many years the whereabouts of Sergeant Prince's war medals was unknown. They were finally recovered at an auction in London, Ontario, and are now held in trust for the Prince family at The Manitoba Museum in Winnipeg. To this day Sergeant Thomas George Prince remains Canada's most decorated Native war hero, and a credit to the chiefs who were his ancestors.

In 1994, to honour Tommy Prince's courage, this monument was installed on the Brokenhead Ojibway Nation Reserve.

Roberta Bondar

The Space Traveller

When Roberta Lynn Bondar was born on December 4, 1945, she came into a world where no one had ever flown in outer space. She grew up in Sault Ste. Marie, Ontario, fascinated by science. The gift of a chemistry set was a real treat, and by the age of seven, she was carrying out experiments in a basement lab her father had built.

Roberta built plastic model rockets. She was also interested in science fiction. She used to pretend that she was part of the cast of the radio program "Flash Gordon," flying to Mars in a rocket ship. "When I was eight years old," she recalls, "to

be a spaceman was the most exciting thing I could imagine." With her older sister, Barbara, she would explore the neighbourhood, pretending to be an astronaut. At night at the family cottage on Lake Superior, she would watch Echo 1, a telecommunications satellite, pass overhead as it orbited Earth, and dream of being up there with it.

"I always thought birds had it over me," she confesses. "They could fly and see the Earth at great distances, and I thought they were beautiful. So it was natural for me to want to fly."

Girl Guides Barbara and Roberta

For Roberta, sports and Girl Guides were just as important as math and science when she was growing up. She attended high school at Sir James Dunn Collegiate and Vocational School in Sault Ste. Marie. She went on to the University of Guelph, then the University of Western Ontario in London, and then the University of Toronto, where she got her Ph.D. Still craving knowledge, she attended medical schools in Canada and the United

In training, Bondar hangs suspended from a parachute harness.

States. She became a neuro-ophthalmologist, a doctor who specializes in how the eye works.

In 1983 Dr. Roberta Bondar applied to the newly formed Canadian Astronaut Program. That December she was one of six Canadian astronauts chosen to train at NASA. It was a tough program. Like the others, she had to ride the "Vomit Comet" to train against motion sickness. Working underwater in a spacesuit helped to prepare her for weightlessness. On January 22, 1992, at 9:52:33 a.m. EST, her dream came true when she and six other crew members left Earth on the space shuttle *Discovery*. Dr. Bondar later would recall that the feeling during liftoff was like being taken by the shoulders and shaken. She wasn't afraid, though. She was far too busy performing the work she had been trained to do.

During the next eight days, as the shuttle orbited Earth 192 times, Roberta Bondar took

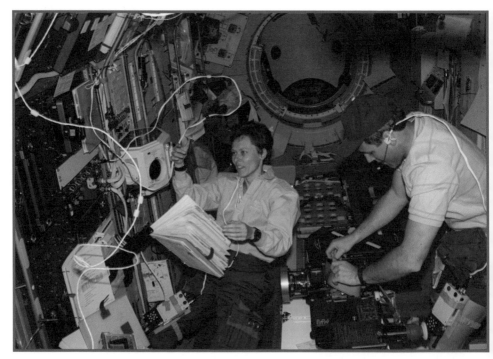

Bondar reviews a checklist in the lab of *Discovery*'s payload bay.

A view of James Bay from the space shuttle

photographs of our planet. In her role as payload specialist, she performed experiments on the effects of weightlessness on the human body. The crew ate tortillas instead of bread to reduce the amount of crumbs floating inside the shuttle, and slept in sleeping bags inside metal cabinets.

Like all space shuttle missions, it was dangerous but very exciting. Looking out into the blackness of outer space, Roberta Bondar became aware of how important Earth was. "I realized that Earth was the only planet that could sustain human life." She later wrote, "The experience changed my life and my attitude toward life itself. I am one of the lucky ones."

The space shuttle returned to Earth on January 30. Roberta Bondar, the first female Canadian astronaut, had been in space for 8 days, 1 hour, 14 minutes and 44 seconds. During her time in space, weightlessness caused her to grow five centimetres, although she did return to her normal height back on Earth. "The most surprising part of flying has to be the landing," she says. "Having not felt our body weight for more than a week, we were all falling over when trying to stand up."

Dr. Roberta Bondar worked for more than a decade at NASA, then set out on new adventures. She is the author of several books, and has been awarded more than 20 honourary degrees from Canadian universities. Several schools have been named after her. She is an Officer of the Order of Canada and has been included in the Canadian

Medical Hall of Fame. In 2005 she began to serve as Chancellor of Trent University in Peterborough, Ontario. Photography continues to be a prime interest. "I'm not comfortable if I'm not learning," says a woman who is still passionate about everything she does, just as she was when she flew bravely into space.

Official portraits of the proud crew of *Discovery*, Cape Canaveral, Florida, 1992

The Fox family: Mom, Dad, 10-year-old Terry on the left, Fred (11½) on the right and Judith (3) and Darrell (6) in front

Terry Fox
The Cancer Fighter

Terrance Stanley Fox. That was the name Betty and Rolly gave to the son born on July 28, 1958, in Winnipeg, Manitoba. Terry spent the next eight years growing up there, with his older brother Fred, younger brother Darrell and baby sister Judith. Their home was a busy place. Rolly was a Canadian National Railway switchman, and Betty was a homemaker, but always the children came first.

Terry, like Fred, attended Wayoata Elementary. School was important, but so was outdoor play in the large field behind their home. Winters were fun, too. Once, the snow drifted so high against the house that the boys could toboggan down it.

Terry, age 9, with a baseball
trophy, and in 1971, third
from right, with his peewee
soccer team

Terry's determined and competitive nature
showed early. At a family picnic softball game, his
nose suddenly began to bleed so badly that he was
taken to hospital. Back at the picnic, he immediately
rejoined the game. No mere nosebleed would stop
Terry Fox.

The Foxes moved to Port Coquitlam, British
Columbia, in 1966, where Terry attended Glen
Elementary and then Mary Hill Junior Secondary
School. He wasn't a natural student, but he studied
hard and did well. Terry met a new friend, Doug
Alward, during grade eight Phys Ed. They played
rugby, baseball and soccer together. They also
competed against each other in cross-country races.

Terry's true goal was to play basketball, but his skills definitely needed improving, so he practised before and after school. Terry and Doug played one-on-one, or "21." By grade ten they were on the Ravens, Port Coquitlam Senior Secondary School's basketball team. "His favourite shot was a spin-a-rama," Doug recalls. "He was a defensive specialist." They shared the Athlete of the Year Award when they graduated.

Terry Fox enrolled at Simon Fraser University in 1976, studying kinesiology, the science of how the body moves. That November he banged his right knee in a car accident. The pain slowly increased until, by spring, it was unbearable. His father drove him to the Royal Columbian Hospital in New Westminster. X-rays were taken. Blood tests and a bone scan were performed. Terry's family gathered supportively around him as the doctor gave them the results. Terry had osteogenic sarcoma, a type of bone cancer. His leg would have to be amputated as soon as possible.

Terry took the news very hard at first but then found the courage to face what was coming. He would lose a leg, but he would never lose his resolve. Six days later Terry's leg was amputated.

The night before the surgery, he read a magazine article about Dick Traum, a one-legged runner who had completed the New York City Marathon. It planted an idea in Terry's mind. He too would run again someday, and when he did, he would run across Canada – to raise money for cancer research.

Within a month he was home and walking with crutches and a temporary prosthesis. He had left the hospital behind, but not the memories of the suffering he had seen there. More determined than ever, he began to train for the greatest challenge of his life. "Nobody is ever going to call me a quitter," he said.

At the invitation of wheelchair athlete Rick Hansen, Terry started to play wheelchair basketball

that summer. "For the entire time he was on the floor," Hansen recalls, "he gave everything he could."

Terry and his team, the Vancouver Cablecars, won the Canadian championship the next year. He began running, and asked Doug for advice. "Start with one lap," Doug told him. That one lap grew and grew. On the Labour Day weekend in 1979, he entered the 17-mile Prince George to Boston Marathon. Three hours and nine minutes later, he finished in last place. He'd never had a greater personal triumph.

Terry was ready. In his day-after-day training, he had run more than 5000 kilometres. The letters he wrote asking

Training every day, Terry gradually builds strength and endurance.

for support were answered. Adidas gave him running shoes, and the Ford Motor Company donated the van Doug would drive. Other companies and organizations were providing money, supplies and support. It was time to run across Canada.

Terry Fox's Marathon of Hope began at St. John's,

Terry Fox waves to the crowd as he runs through Toronto on his Marathon of Hope.

Newfoundland, on April 12, 1980. With CBC filming, he dipped his artificial leg into the Atlantic Ocean. He began to run.

Canadians watched his now familiar step-step-stride as he pushed on across Nova Scotia, Prince Edward Island and New Brunswick, where his brother Darrell joined him. "His smile is what I remember most that day," Darrell recalls.

The country responded. In Montreal, Quebec, businessman Isadore Sharp organized a fundraiser.

Children gave change, people cheered, and Canada pitched in as Terry Fox ran through Ontario. Terry began to think big – one dollar from every Canadian for cancer research. "If you've given a dollar," he said in one of his many speeches, "you are part of the Marathon of Hope."

A shoe worn by Terry Fox during his run across Canada

Terry Fox touched the lives of many young people. In northern Ontario, he spent time with Greg Scott, a ten-year-old boy who also had lost a leg to cancer.

Then, just outside Thunder Bay, Terry began coughing. His chest hurt so much that he asked Doug to drive him to a hospital. The tests told Terry what he had suspected, that

cancer was now in his lungs. Rolly and Betty Fox flew to Ontario to bring their son home for more

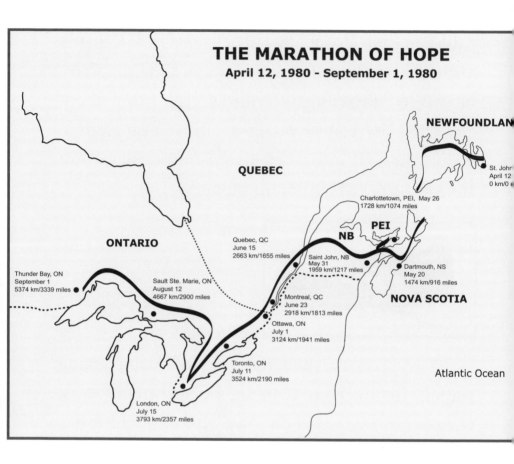

THE MARATHON OF HOPE
April 12, 1980 - September 1, 1980

NEWFOUNDLAND

QUEBEC

St. John'
April 12
0 km/0

Charlottetown, PEI, May 26
1728 km/1074 miles

PEI
NB

ONTARIO

Quebec, QC
June 15
2663 km/1655 miles

Saint John, NB
May 31
1959 km/1217 miles

Dartmouth, NS
May 20
1474 km/916 miles

Thunder Bay, ON
September 1
5374 km/3339 miles

Sault Ste. Marie, ON
August 12
4667 km/2900 miles

Montreal, QC
June 23
2918 km/1813 miles

NOVA SCOTIA

Ottawa, ON
July 1
3124 km/1941 miles

Toronto, ON
July 11
3524 km/2190 miles

Atlantic Ocean

London, ON
July 15
3793 km/2357 miles

treatment. He had run 5374 kilometres in those 143 days, and he was determined to finish. "I promise I won't give up," he told Canadians that afternoon at a press conference. "I hope that what I've done has been an inspiration."

It was. The next day Isadore Sharp tele-grammed, promising to organize a run held each year in Terry Fox's name. On September 7 Terry watched a CTV fundraising broadcast as he underwent more chemotherapy in hospital. Ten and a half million dollars was raised, but it didn't stop there. Thousands of people wrote or telegrammed, as dances, recitals, run-a-thons and walk-a-thons were held. By February 1981 more than twenty-four million dollars had been raised. His courage was inspiring the world.

For months Terry Fox fought the hardest battle of his life, and he was even able to return home for a while. He never gave up his dream of finishing the Marathon of Hope. But on June 28, 1981, with his family around him, Terry Fox died. Flags on all Canadian federal buildings were lowered to half staff. He was laid to rest at Port Coquitlam cemetery,

This monument near Thunder Bay marks the end of Terry Fox's cross-country run.

Terry Fox runs along the Trans-Canada Highway in northern Ontario, escorted by police.

while his loved ones and all of Canada mourned.

Terry Fox was honoured during his brief life. He was the youngest Canadian to be named a Companion of the Order of Canada. He was awarded B.C.'s highest civilian award, the Order of the Dogwood. Since his death, parks, monuments, schools, a B.C. mountain, and an icebreaker have been named after him. In 1999, in a national survey, he was voted Canada's greatest hero.

And every September since his death, The Terry Fox Run has taken place all over the world. The Terry Fox Foundation has given hundreds of millions of dollars toward cancer research. Terry Fox once wrote, "Somewhere the hurting must stop." Until that day comes, this heroic Canadian's Marathon of Hope will continue.